DETROIT RED WINGS

BY BRENDAN FLYNN

Book design by Maggie Villaume
Cover design by Maggie Villaume

Photographs ©: Paul Sancya/AP Images, cover, 4–5; Gene J. Puskar/AP Images, 7; Frank Gunn/The Canadian Press/AP Images, 9, 24–25; AP Images, 10–11, 15; Preston Stroup/AP Images, 13; Alvin Quinn/AP Images, 17; Al Messerschmidt/AP Images, 18–19; Jeff Mcintosh/CP/AP Images, 21; Tom Pidgeon/AP Images, 22–23; Derik Hamilton/AP Images, 27; Duane Burleson/AP Images, 28

Press Box Books, an imprint of Press Room Editions.

ISBN
978-1-63494-491-5 (library bound)
978-1-63494-517-2 (paperback)
978-1-63494-568-4 (epub)
978-1-63494-543-1 (hosted ebook)

Library of Congress Control Number: 2022902275

Distributed by North Star Editions, Inc.
2297 Waters Drive
Mendota Heights, MN 55120
www.northstareditions.com

Printed in the United States of America
082022

ABOUT THE AUTHOR

Brendan Flynn is a San Francisco resident and an author of numerous children's books. In addition to writing about sports, Flynn also enjoys competing in triathlons, Scrabble tournaments, and chili cook-offs.

TABLE OF CONTENTS

1

Henrik Zetterberg rips a shot in the 2008 Stanley Cup Final.

GOING FOR NUMBER 11

*T*he fans were roaring at Pittsburgh's Mellon Arena. Their Penguins were hosting the Detroit Red Wings in Game 6 of the 2008 Stanley Cup Final. Detroit led the series three games to two. But Pittsburgh had just won Game 5 in Detroit. Winning on their home ice would force a Game 7.

The Red Wings had the best record in the National Hockey

League (NHL) that season. Much of their success was due to their offensive talent. They put that skill on display early in the first period.

On a power play, forward Pavel Datsyuk gathered a loose puck along the boards. Datsyuk scanned the ice for options. He passed to teammate Henrik Zetterberg. Zetterberg looked across the ice and saw defenseman Brian Rafalski. Rafalski blasted a wrist shot at the top of the face-off circle. The puck rocketed past Penguins goalie Marc-André Fleury. The Red Wings were off to a great start.

Detroit led 2–1 in the third period when Zetterberg struck again. This time he took a shot that trickled between

Brian Rafalski celebrates with the bench after his goal in Game 6.

Fleury's leg pads. The puck found its way

into the net for a 3–1 Red Wings lead.

The Penguins didn't give up, though.

Late in the third period, they scored a

power play goal of their own. That made the score 3–2. As the clock ticked down toward zero, Pittsburgh took one last shot. But Detroit goalie Chris Osgood made a save in the game's final second. The buzzer sounded. The Red Wings had won the Stanley Cup!

The title was Detroit's 11th Stanley Cup. Only two teams in NHL history have won more.

LOOK OUT BELOW!

Red Wings fans enjoy one of the most unusual traditions in all of sports. During playoff games, Detroit fans throw octopuses onto the ice to celebrate goals. The tradition started in 1952. An owner of a fish market celebrated a Red Wings goal by tossing an octopus over the boards. An octopus has eight tentacles. And at the time, teams needed eight wins to lift the Stanley Cup.

Nicklas Lidström lifts the Stanley Cup and celebrates with his teammates.

2

Ted Lindsay
served as
Detroit's captain
in the mid-1950s.

FIND YOUR WINGS

Detroit entered the NHL in 1926. However, the team wasn't called the Red Wings back then. The team was originally called the Detroit Cougars. But the city of Detroit didn't have a suitable arena. So, the Cougars played their home games across the border in Windsor, Ontario, Canada. One year later, Olympia Stadium opened in downtown Detroit. That was where the team would play for the next five decades.

In 1932, the team settled on the Red Wings name. Championships soon followed. The Wings won their first two Stanley Cups in 1936 and 1937. They were led by center Marty Barry. The veteran was the team's leading scorer in both of those seasons.

Detroit won another Cup in 1943. That set the stage for a long run of success.

THE WINGED WHEEL

After changing its name to the Red Wings in 1932, the team needed a new logo. Team owner James Norris had played for a team called the Winged Wheelers in Montreal. So, he modified that team's logo. His new version showed a red wheel with two wings emerging from it. The Red Wings have used the logo ever since.

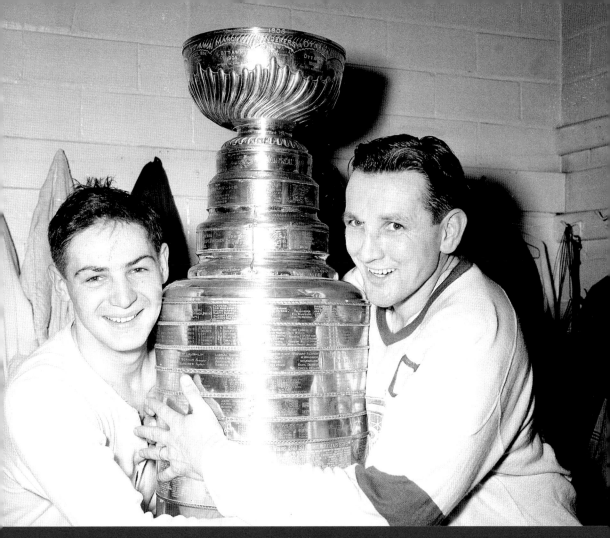

Sid Abel (right) and Terry Sawchuck celebrate with the Cup in 1952.

Beginning in 1949, the Red Wings finished in first place seven seasons in a row. During that time, they won four Stanley Cups. The team was led by the

"Production Line." This group featured center Sid Abel, left wing Ted Lindsay, and right wing Gordie Howe.

In 1950, those three players were the top three scorers in the league. Lindsay's 78 points led the way. The 21-year-old Howe was injured in the playoffs. But his teammates stepped up. Detroit beat the New York Rangers in double overtime in Game 7 to win the Cup. In 1952, Howe led the Red Wings to another Cup. This time they swept the Montreal Canadiens. Detroit added two more Cup titles in 1954 and 1955.

The Red Wings made the Final five more times in the next 11 seasons. However, they came home empty-handed

Goalie Terry Sawchuck gets lifted up by his teammates after a win.

each year. That was the start of a long
drought for Detroit hockey fans. But it
only made what was to come that much
sweeter.

GORDIE HOWE

Gordie Howe was so important to the sport that he earned the nickname "Mr. Hockey." The longtime star joined Detroit in 1946 when he was 18 years old. He didn't hang up his Red Wings uniform until 1971. For 25 seasons, the Saskatchewan native used his strength, skill, and toughness to dominate the league.

Howe led the NHL in scoring six times. And he finished in the top five for 21 straight seasons. Howe was a six-time league most valuable player (MVP). He played in 22 All-Star Games. When he retired, he was the NHL's all-time leader in goals and assists.

One of his lasting legacies is the "Gordie Howe hat trick." That title describes when a player has a goal, an assist, and a fight in the same game. While it is named after Howe, he did it only twice in his career.

Gordie Howe (right) celebrates with his teammates after scoring his 544th goal, tying the NHL record.

3

Steve Yzerman
has the most
assists (1,063)
in Red Wings
history.

RETURN TO
GLORY

After losing the 1966 Stanley Cup Final, the Red Wings struggled to compete. Their veteran stars began retiring. The youngsters replacing them had a hard time filling their skates. From 1967 to 1983, the Red Wings made the playoffs just twice.

But in the mid-1980s, Detroit began turning things around. Head coach Jacques Demers led the team to the conference finals in

1987 and 1988. Young players like centers Steve Yzerman and Adam Oates began to give fans hope.

In 1993, the Wings hired Scotty Bowman to take over as head coach. Bowman had guided the Canadiens to five Stanley Cups in the 1970s. He won another one with the Penguins in 1992.

By 1995–96, the Wings had built a machine. Yzerman and Sergei Fedorov

STEVE YZERMAN

Steve Yzerman defined leadership for 22 years in Detroit. In 1986, the 21-year-old center became the youngest captain in team history. He wore the C on his Red Wings jersey for the next 19 seasons. A strong two-way player, Yzerman won the Conn Smythe Trophy as the playoff MVP in 1998. He went on to a successful career in the front office of the Red Wings. Yzerman was inducted into the Hockey Hall of Fame in 2009.

tormented opposing defenders. Nicklas Lidström and Vladimir Konstantinov stood strong in front of Chris Osgood in net. The Red Wings finished with 131 points that season. They were just one point behind Bowman's 1976–77 Canadiens for the best of all time.

However, those Wings were upset by the Colorado Avalanche in the conference finals. Fans in Detroit began to wonder whether they'd ever see the Stanley Cup again.

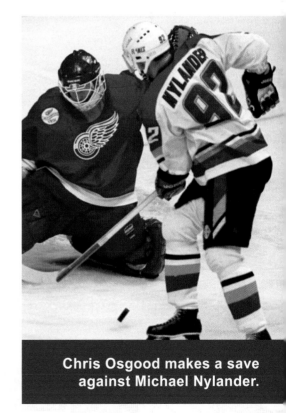

Chris Osgood makes a save against Michael Nylander.

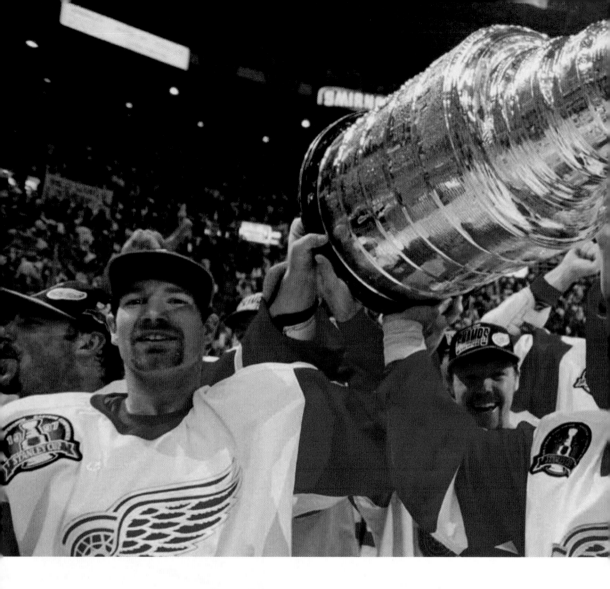

They didn't have anything to worry about. In 1997, the Red Wings swept the Philadelphia Flyers in the Stanley Cup Final. It was their first championship in 42 years. And they didn't wait long to

The Red Wings celebrate winning the 1997 Stanley Cup.

win another one. In 1998, they swept the Washington Capitals to win their second straight Cup. They added another title in 2002. And their 2008 championship was their fourth in 11 seasons.

4

Nicklas
Lidström
hangs his head
after losing
Game 7 of
the 2009
Stanley Cup.

THE STREAK
ENDS

Red Wings fans had grown used to success again. They returned to the Stanley Cup Final in 2009. This time, the Penguins won the title. Detroit regularly made the playoffs after that. But another drought tested the patience of the team's supporters.

The Red Wings found themselves on the sidelines

when the 2017 playoffs began. It was the first time they had missed the playoffs in 25 years. Through the 2020–21 season, they had yet to make it back. Detroit hit rock bottom in the 2019–20 season. The Red Wings finished with only 39 points in 71 games. They had the worst record in the league by far. In fact, it was the team's worst season since 1985–86, when Detroit finished with 40 points in 80 games.

Even so, Red Wings fans had hope for the future. The team's struggles resulted in many high draft picks. And the Wings used those picks on skilled players. Left wing Lucas Raymond was taken fourth overall in the 2020 draft. He made his debut in 2021 at 19 years old. Raymond

Lucas Raymond skates toward the goal against the Philadelphia Flyers.

was joined by 20-year-old defenseman Moritz Seider. He was the sixth pick in the 2019 draft.

Dylan Larkin celebrates scoring against the Devils.

Those prospects joined a roster with more experienced young players. Center Dylan Larkin played six full seasons before turning 25. Winger Tyler Bertuzzi and defenseman Filip Hronek both made their debuts before turning 22. The front office compiled a bunch of young talent. Red Wings fans hoped this core would lead the team to its next dynasty.

JOE LOUIS ARENA

For 38 years, the Red Wings called Joe Louis Arena home. It was named after the legendary boxer from Detroit. Louis was the heavyweight champion for 12 years. The Wings experienced similar success while playing in the arena named after him. They made the Stanley Cup Final six times while playing there, winning four times. The name of the arena never changed for 38 years. The Red Wings moved into Little Caesars Arena at the start of the 2017–18 season.

• DETROIT RED WINGS
QUICK STATS

TEAM HISTORY: Detroit Cougars (1926–30), Detroit Falcons (1930–32), Detroit Red Wings (1932–)

STANLEY CUP CHAMPIONSHIPS: 11 (1936, 1937, 1943, 1950, 1952, 1954, 1955, 1997, 1998, 2002, 2008)

KEY COACHES:

- Jack Adams (1927–47): 327 wins, 290 losses, 123 ties

- Scotty Bowman (1993–2002): 410 wins, 193 losses, 88 ties, 10 overtime losses

- Mike Babcock (2005–15): 458 wins, 223 losses, 105 overtime losses

HOME ARENA: Little Caesars Arena (Detroit, MI)

MOST CAREER POINTS: Gordie Howe (1,809)

MOST CAREER GOALS: Gordie Howe (786)

MOST CAREER ASSISTS: Steve Yzerman (1,063)

MOST CAREER SHUTOUTS: Terry Sawchuk (85)

Stats are accurate through the 2020–21 season.

GLOSSARY

CONFERENCE
A subset of teams within a sports league.

DEBUT
First appearance.

DRAFT
An event that allows teams to choose new players coming into the league.

FACE-OFF
The start or a restart of play, in which the referee drops the puck between two opposing players.

FORWARD
A left wing, center, or right wing.

PLAYOFFS
A set of games to decide a league's champion.

POINT
Players earn points for goals and assists. Teams earn two points in the standings for a victory and one point for an overtime or shoot-out loss.

POWER PLAY
A situation in which one team has more players on the ice because an opposing player is serving a penalty.

TO LEARN MORE

BOOKS

Berglund, Bruce. *Big-Time Hockey Records*. North Mankato, MN: Capstone Press, 2022.

Ferrell, Giles. *Great Hockey Debates*. Minneapolis: Abdo Publishing, 2019.

Martin, Brett S. *STEM in Hockey*. Minneapolis: Abdo Publishing, 2018.

MORE INFORMATION

To learn more about the Detroit Red Wings, go to **pressboxbooks.com/AllAccess**.

These links are routinely monitored and updated to provide the most current information available.

INDEX